FAVOURITE ROSES

PETER HARKNESS
FAVOURITE
ROSES

150 Garden Classics

WARD LOCK

PUBLISHER'S NOTE
The names of roses vary from country to country, and sometimes even within a country. The roses in this book are listed under the name they are mainly known by in Great Britain, but their alternative names are also given. Where applicable, the patent name of a variety has been included. These are recognisable by the three capital letters at the beginning of the name; e.g., MACeye is the patent name for the rose 'Eyepaint', bred by Sam McGredy. At any particular time certain rose varieties are unavailable through nurseries and garden centres; a new variety may not have been released, or older varieties may not be currently popular. The author has, however, endeavoured to ensure that most of these roses are available.

PHOTOGRAPHY CREDITS
Geoff Bryant pages 10, 11, 13, 14, 15, 16(top), 17, 18, 19, 20, 22, 24, 25, 27, 28, 30, 31, 32, 33(top), 34, 36, 37, 38, 39(bottom), 42, 43, 44, 46, 47, 48, 49, 51, 53, 55, 56, 57(top), 58, 61(left), 63, 64, 67, 68, 69, 70, 72, 73, 77, 78(left), 80, 81, 82, 83(bottom), 84, 85, 87(top), 88, 90(top), 92(right), 93, 95, 96, 100, 101(left), 103, 104, 105, 106, 107, 108, 109, 110, 111, 113, 115, 116, 117(bottom), 118, 125, 126(top); Dawn and Barry Eagle 123(top); Peter and Betty Harkness pages 8, 9, 12, 21, 23, 26, 29, 33(bottom), 35, 40, 41, 50, 52, 57, 59, 61(right), 62, 65(top), 66, 71, 74, 75, 76, 78(right), 79, 83(top), 86, 87(bottom), 89, 90(bottom), 91, 92(left), 94, 97, 98, 101, 102, 112, 114, 117(top), 119, 120, 121, 122, 123(bottom), 124(bottom), 126(bottom); FB Notcutts Nurseries page 39(top); V Page pages 54, 65(bottom); RNRS page 124(top); Terry Wood pages 45, 99

FRONT COVER: "Many Happy Returns", detail "High Hopes"
BACK COVER (from left): "Compassion", "Zonta", "City Girl"

A WARD LOCK BOOK

Ward Lock
Wellington House, 125 Strand
London WC2R OBB
A Cassell Imprint

Copyright © David Bateman Limited, 1996

First published in Great Britain 1996
in association with
David Bateman Limited
Tarndale Grove, Albany Business Park, Bush Road
Albany, Auckland, New Zealand

British Library Cataloguing in Publication Data
A Catalogue record for this book is available from the British
Library

ISBN 0 7063 7494 0

Printed in Hong Kong by Colorcraft Limited

CONTENTS

INTRODUCTION — ROSES FOR ALL

Roses for all? Well, to be honest, not quite all. When a survey was carried out in Britain not long ago, it was found that two per cent of the population said they hated roses. As an ardent rose fan, even I have had moments of disenchantment — while pruning, say, or wrestling with deep-seated suckers — but such feelings are far eclipsed by the pleasure of a rose's flower and fragrance, and the fascination of its manifold (and still evolving) forms. And after all, if ninety-eight per cent of us are agreed on something, it must have a great deal going for it.

What is it that makes the rose so special? So special, that from the combined nurseries of the world we can buy more than 10,000 different kinds. So special, that it has been used in many cultures to suit almost every decorative purpose you can imagine. So special, that it is the most universally adopted national flower, recognised by England, Honduras, Iran, Poland, Romania, Slovakia — and more recently by the USA, where as a State symbol it also belongs to Georgia, Iowa, New York, North Dakota and the District of Columbia.

The decision to proclaim the rose as 'The National Floral Emblem of the USA' came when Ronald Regan was President, and only after decades of arguing, in the course of which some seventy bills had been introduced in Congress in support of a variety of flowers. As well as the rose, those petitioned for included the marigold, dogwood, daffodil, daisy, sunflower, orchid and carnation.The only serious challenger in the final stages was the marigold, but, as someone said, 'Whoever presented his girl with marigolds?'

These are wonderful achievements, and the claims of the rose do not end there. What other plant family can match its versatility, from the miniature around our ankles to the climber fifty feet up a tree outlined against the sky?

What can better its continuity of bloom, from early spring to late winter, if we plant the right varieties? Or its colour palette, with virtually every shade save blue and black, and many multicolours? Or the diversity of flower shapes, and arrangements of petals, which may number from four to a hundred or more? Or the rapid evolution of new forms, thanks to the dedication of plant breeders — now joined by biotechnologists — of many nations? Roses as garden plants are quick to establish and slow to die. No wonder we all (well, ninety-eight per cent of us) love them.

The rose carries a deeper symbolism too, sensed and expressed by writers and poets down the ages. It arises from the paradox of beauty emerging, so incongruously, from a nest of thorns. Edmund Spenser summarised it in nine words:

Sweet is the rose, but grows upon a brier

The poets perceive the coexistence of pleasure and pain and find in the rose a powerful symbol of this; powerful because of its truth in human experience. We cannot expect birth without pain, joys without sorrows, life without death. (And who among us does not have an ingrained feeling that medicine, to do us good, should taste unpleasant?)

These thoughts were in the mind of Britain's Nigel Hawthorne when he was asked to explain his love of roses. He summed it up in words that surely cannot be bettered.

Roses seem to epitomise the brevity of life and yet in that all-too-brief and glorious flowering they are truly magnificent. It's such an unfair standard for the rest of us to emulate.

In this book are 150 of my favourite roses. I hope that you may have the chance to enjoy their 'glorious flowering' not just on these pages, but in your garden or a garden near you. I have written it for everyone who counts roses among the many good things that life has to offer.

Peter Harkness

SPECIES AND OLD GARDEN ROSES

ALBA MAXIMA   *R. x ALBA MAXIMA*, CHESHIRE ROSE, GREAT WHITE ROSE, JACOBITE ROSE

Alba shrub

This is one of the great historic roses of the West, so vigorous that it grows readily on its own roots and can survive decades of neglect. Its upright habit and grey-green leaves make it distinctive even when not in flower. The clear white blooms, filled with short petals and sweetly scented, appear in profusion in midsummer. Established plants will reach 2.2 x 1.5 m (7 x 5 ft).

'Maxima' is assumed to have had an ancient five-petalled ancestor, and to have evolved down the centuries through spontaneous fuller-petalled forms being selected by gardeners. It enters history in its heraldic five-petalled form, as the badge of the fourteenth-century Earls of March. It came to be linked to the Royal House of York about the year 1410, through the marriage of the March heiress, Anne Mortimer, to Richard, son of Edmund of Langley, Duke of York.

The name 'Jacobite Rose' links it to the exiled King James II who died in 1701, and who, as Duke of York, had the white rose as his badge. The white rose continued for many years to symbolise rebellion in Scotland against English rule. Introduced fifteenth century or earlier.

Alba Maxima

Canary Bird

CANARY BIRD

Wild rose hybrid shrub

Small, single, yellow, lightly scented blooms are borne along the stems. The special joy of this rose is that they appear in springtime, usually before any other rose, heralding in a most cheerful way all the pleasures to come. There is often a spasmodic token of late season flower, but the whole aspect of the plant, with its dense shrub habit, fine ferny leaves and reddish stems is such that, in flower or not, it remains a credit to the garden. It does need space, reaching 3 x 4 m (9 x 12 ft). There is some question as to whether it came to Britain direct from China in 1907, as seed from a similar Chinese species, or was a botanic garden selection raised subsequently and passed around. Sources in the US are unfortunately limited.

Cécile Brunner, climbing

CÉCILE BRUNNER, CLIMBING

Polyantha climber

A vigorous climbing form of a charming old polyantha with petite pink blooms like miniature hybrid teas. It is of value to the flower arranger for the succession of perfect buds produced from early summer to late autumn, and recommended where there is space – it suits a high wall or fence, pergola or tree. 4 x 4 m (12 x 12 ft).
HOSP 1894.

CHARLES DE MILLS BIZARRE TRIOMPHANT

Gallica shrub

A most strange rose, with flowers that look, when open, as if someone has sliced the tops off with a knife. They appear as pink buds, then open to large, fragrant, beetroot-purple blooms crammed with infolded petals. (The books often say 'quartered', but as you examine the flower, 'sixteenthed' seems more like it.) This lovely dark-leaved rose flowers in summer only, on bushy, rather top-heavy plants, 1.2 m (4 ft) tall and wide; it can do with some support. Its name sounds peculiarly Anglo-French but the origin of this rose is not known.

Charles de Mills

Common Moss

COMMON MOSS COMMUNIS, OLD PINK MOSS, R. x *CENTIFOLIA MUSCOSA*

Moss shrub

This ancient rose of many aliases has delighted generations of rose lovers since the early eighteenth century. It is a sport of the pink centifolia rose, with very full, richly scented flowers, and a dainty covering of so-called 'moss' over the flower buds and stems. It flowers in summertime and a support for the plant is useful, as the heavy flowers weigh down the branches. Grows to 1.5 x 1.4 m (5 x 4 ft). Found in France about 1700.

Complicata

COMPLICATA

Gallica shrub

This is not at all typical of gallica roses, as it bears large, pink, pale-centred flowers of five petals. They appear in summer on huge plants which branch out strongly to 2.2 x 2.5 m (7 x 8 ft), with large greyish-green leaves. Why does a simple rose like this have the name 'Complicata'? The best explanation seems to be that complicata means, botanically, a fold, and some of the petal edges often have a folded appearance. The origin of this rose is unknown; perhaps it has some *R. canina* or *R. macrantha* in it.

Comte de Chambord

COMTE DE CHAMBORD

Portland shrub

The Portland roses are a small group combining the genes of roses from East and West This variety has a pretty old-fashioned quartered shape and the ability to continue in bloom into autumn. The scent is good and the greyish-green leaves attractive. It is neater in growth than most old shrub roses, and therefore well suited to smaller modern gardens. Normally it grows to 1.2 x 1 m (48 x 36 in).
ROBERT & MOREAU 1860.

Cramoisi Supérieur

CRAMOISI SUPÉRIEUR AGRIPPINA, LADY BRISBANE

China shrub

This was a great novelty in the early nineteenth century, when crimson roses were arriving in the West. It bears big clusters of small double blooms, flowers through summer and autumn, and the growth is bushy and open, sometimes spindly, but very responsive to climate. In mild conditions it will keep extending well beyond the normal 75 x 120 cm (30 x 48 in) which most gardeners can expect. It has typical China leaves, small, pointed and shiny.
COQUEREAU 1832.

DUPONTII   *R. MOSCHATA NIVEA*, SNOWBUSH ROSE

Wild rose hybrid shrub

This ancient rose covers itself in summer with fragrant creamy-white flowers showing yellow anthers. They stand out beautifully against greyish-green leaves on a strong upright plant up to 2.2 m (7 ft) tall and wide. The rose bears the name of André Dupont, founder of the famous rose collection in the Luxembourg Gardens in Paris. May have *R. moschata*, *R. gallica* and an Alba rose in its ancestry, and dates from before 1817. Only very limited availability in the US.

Dupontii

FANTIN-LATOUR

Centifolia shrub

Fantin-Latour

Unmistakably a beauty, with fragrant rose-pink blooms of medium to large size, full of intricate petal folds, and maintaining a lovely circular outline as they expand. It flowers with amazing generosity in summer, on a dark-leafed, spreading, open, strong shrub, 1.5 x 1.2 m (5 x 4 ft) or more. The smooth leaves indicate some China parentage, so it is not one of the ancient Centifolias. Apart from that its origin is unknown. Graham Thomas relates that the name by which it has come to be known was thought up by Mrs Ruby Fleischmann, who had it as an unnamed rose from Mrs Messel of Nymans in Sussex, where it had been established many years. Mrs Fleischmann gave it the artist's name because of its resemblance to roses in his paintings. The date often assigned to it of 'circa 1900' is an informed guess.

Ispahan

ISPAHAN POMPON DES PRINCES, ROSE D'ISFAHAN

Damask shrub

The origin of this old rose is a mystery, but its name reminds us of the debt owed by rose lovers to the people of Persia, who have grown and cherished it for untold years. It has abundant and attractive greyish-green foliage, and bears a generous harvest of fragrant, clear pink blooms over a long period in summer. The flowers, as Michael Gibson has pointed out, look fuller of petals than they are. The plant can extend to 180 x 90 cm (6 x 3 ft) if given support, or can be left to form a lax shrub. It has been known to Europe since 1832, and is reputed to have been used in Turkey for distilling rose water.

Kazanlik

KAZANLIK   *R. DAMASCENA TRIGINTIPETALA*

Damask shrub

This is the celebrated rose used extensively to make attar of roses, taking its name from a district in Bulgaria perfectly suited to its cultivation, with tall mountains to the north to cut out cold winds, and low hills to the south to create a sun trap. In the garden it can take up considerable space, bearing fragrant, rather loosely formed flowers in mid to deep pink shades on a vigorous plant up to 2.2 x 2 m (7 x 6 ft). It is a damask of the older type, flowering in summer only. No doubt it has an oriental origin, and may be related to varieties grown in Turkey, Saudi Arabia and Iran for similar cosmetic reasons. In cultivation before 1850.

MME ISAAC PEREIRE

Bourbon shrub or climber

The strong purplish-pink colour may not be to everyone's taste, but this old rose has survived through its vigour, hardiness, fragrance and delightful form of the flowers. They are filled with petals, opening cupped and quartered, often in clusters too heavy for the stems. For this reason the plant looks best on a support. The first blooms may be misshapen due to the effects of cold spring weather. The growth is open and rather lax to 2.2 x 2 m (7 x 6 ft). It was named for the wife of a Parisian banker. GARÇON 1881.

Mme Isaac Pereire

Mutabilis

Old Blush

MUTABILIS *R. CHINENSIS* MUTABILIS, TIPO IDEALE

China shrub or climber

'The countless blossoms resemble flights of butterflies' was
Graham Thomas's comment on this rose. The five-petalled flowers
change colour in an amazing way, from light yellow to pink to
slate purple. The blooms appear quite early in summer, and
continue until autumn. The leaves are shiny and plum coloured,
giving perfunctory cover on spindly plants of 1.2 x 1 m (4 x 3 ft)
or up to 3 x 2 m (10 x 6 ft) on walls protected from cold winds.
The name 'Mutabilis', the Latin word for 'changeable', is said to
have been given to this rose by the Swiss gardener Henri
Correvon, who received it as a gift from Italy in the 1890s. How
and when it arrived there is a mystery.

OLD BLUSH COMMON BLUSH CHINA, MONTHLY ROSE, PARSON'S PINK

China bush

This was the sensation of the later eighteenth century because of its ability to flower from summer until forced into dormancy by late season frosts. The pink flowers open loosely, in well spaced clusters, and shiny, pointed leaves (a novelty in the Europe of the 1750s) cover the plant. The amount of growth varies according to climate: 90 x 75 cm (36 x 30 in) may be expected in Britain, but two or three times as much in frost-free Bermuda. This Chinese garden rose is said to have come to Europe in 1752.

QUATRE SAISONS AUTUMN DAMASK, FOUR SEASONS, DAMASCENA BIFERA, *R. DAMASCENA SEMPERFLORENS*, ROSE OF CASTILLE

Damask shrub

As the names imply, this is famous for its ability to give late season flower, something unheard of in Europe when it was introduced. The fragrant flowers are pink, loosely formed, borne in clusters during summer, and fitfully thereafter until autumn. The plants carry downy foliage and make lanky, arching growth to 1.5 x 1.2 m (5 x 4 ft).

This is thought to be a cross between *R. gallica* and *R. moschata* (though in place of the last named, *R. abyssinica* has recently been suggested by Ivan Louette of Belgium as more likely, because, unlike *R. moschata*, it repeats its flower). It was mentioned in Italy in 1633, but is probably much older and of Middle Eastern origin.

Quatre Saisons

ROSA FOETIDA AUSTRIAN BRIAR, AUSTRIAN YELLOW, *R. LUTEA*

Wild shrub rose

This brightest of yellows bears its saucer-shaped five-petalled flowers very early in the season, festooned along the branches against chocolate-brown stems. It has small, shiny serrated leaves and an upright, arching habit, with twiggy stems, to 1.5 m (5 ft) high and wide. Sometimes it will die back, and black spot is likely later in the season.

Its importance in rose history is indicated by the various names. Lutea means yellow, and was its earlier species name, but this was changed to R. foetida in reference to its pungent and unpleasing fragrance. 'Austrian Yellow' recalls a stage on its journey from Turkey across Europe in the sixteenth century, though there is reason to believe the Spaniards had it much earlier than that, via Africa. Its home is western Asia, and they say the petals are used by jam makers in Iraq.

Rosa foetida

ROSA GALLICA *R. RUBRA*

Rosa gallica

The scented, five-petalled flowers are reddish pink, admitting much variation from rose pink to near crimson. They open flat to 6 cm (2.5 in) across, which is larger than most species, and continue in flower for several weeks. Gallica roses extend by suckering, and can colonise a wide area; one may expect an individual plant to grow 1 m (40 in) high and wide. The bushes carry characteristic gallica foliage, darkish green, with a matt surface, and rough to the touch. Their native habitat extends across southern Europe to the Near East.

The form *R. gallica officinalis* ('Apothecary's Rose', 'Officinalis', 'Provins Rose', 'Red Damask', 'Red Rose of Lancaster', *R. provincialis*) provides more fully petalled blooms. These have been the delight of gardeners, herbalists and cosmeticians since ancient times. The plant makes a neat, fairly rounded shrub, 80 x 90 cm (32 x 36 in), flowering over several weeks of summer, and perhaps came to Europe from the Near East in the thirteenth century.

ROSA NITIDA

Wild shrub rose

This is perhaps an improved form of the wild rose, and its compact spreading habit and shiny red-tinted leaves appeal to plantsmen. It tolerates dampish soil and is often planted in association with ornamental ponds. The single, bright lilac-rose blooms appear in summer on bristly, reddish stems, are scented, and succeeded by red hips. It grows 60 x 90 cm (2 x 3 ft) but will extend itself by suckering. Its native habitat is in eastern North America and it has been known to cultivation since 1807.

Rosa nitida

Rosa pimpinellifolia altaica

ROSA PIMPINELLIFOLIA ALTAICA

Scots shrub

The name refers to the Altai mountains in Central Asia, whence this was brought to the knowledge of gardeners in 1818. It is one of the hardiest and toughest roses, ideal for planting schemes where it can largely fend for itself. The scented, saucer-shaped creamy-white flowers are quite large for a species, 6 cm (2.5 in) across, very noticeable in early summer on upright, shrubby plants to 2 x 1.2 m (6 x 4 ft). The leaves are small and dark.

ROSA PIMPINELLIFOLIA IRISH RICH MARBLED

Scots shrub

Nothing seems to be known of the origin of this pretty rose. Light pink buds open to show irregular patterns of deeper pink, with a hint of lilac. The flowers are loosely formed, scented, and like other Scots roses they appear early in summer. The leaflets are small, dark and burnet-like with serrated edges, giving good cover on spreading, suckering plants up to 1 m (36 in) in height.

Rosa pimpinellifolia Irish Rich Marbled

Rosa rugosa rubra

ROSA RUGOSA RUBRA HEDGEHOG ROSE, JAPANESE ROSE, RAMANAS ROSE

Wild shrub rose

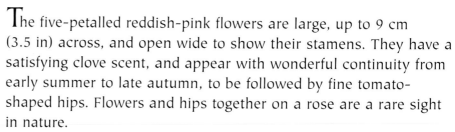

The five-petalled reddish-pink flowers are large, up to 9 cm (3.5 in) across, and open wide to show their stamens. They have a satisfying clove scent, and appear with wonderful continuity from early summer to late autumn, to be followed by fine tomato-shaped hips. Flowers and hips together on a rose are a rare sight in nature.

As befits the 'Hedgehog Rose', the habit is compact and very leafy, up to 1.5 m (5 ft) high and wide. The leaves are leathery and wrinkled (which is what 'rugose' means). Closely related forms with wine-red, pink, white, and purple flowers all share the same characteristics. They will naturalise themselves quite happily, but their original habitats are the coastal areas of China, Korea and Japan. From Japan it was brought to Europe in 1796 and later; it is known there as 'Hama-nasu', of which the name 'Ramanas Rose' is no doubt a corruption.

Rose de Rescht

ROSE DE RESCHT

Damask shrub

The rich magenta-pink colour, pretty form and good scent make this a particular favourite, and it is useful for those who have smaller gardens, for growth is manageable and compact, with good leaf cover, to 90 x 75 cm (36 x 30 in). Like many damasks, it extends its flowering through summer and autumn. It takes its name from a city in Persia and was brought to Europe by Nancy Lindsay in the 1940s.

Souvenir de St Anne's

SOUVENIR DE ST ANNE'S

Bourbon shrub

The pearly blush blooms have few petals, but they make the most of them, opening out wide to telling effect on dark-foliaged, shrubby plants. They are scented, and continue flowering from summer through to autumn. Jack Harkness said of this rose that 'it could well be taken as the emblem of purity'.

The variety grows to about 1.5 x 1.2 m (5 x 4 ft) and is said to be a sport of an extremely full-petalled rose, 'Souvenir de la Malmaison'. It was grown in Ireland for many years (St Anne's being a famous garden at Clontarf), and introduced, through the agency of Graham Thomas, by Hilling in 1950.

Versicolor

VERSICOLOR *R. GALLICA VERSICOLOR,* ROSA MUNDI

Gallica shrub

Since the seventeenth century, perhaps earlier, this has been a firm favourite, because of curious random striping on the petals. They appear to be deep pink-striped blush, though the truth is that this 'striping' occurs where the colour pigment is missing. The rose is a sport of R. gallica officinalis, with similar characteristics of flowering and growth.

The rose was mentioned in Europe in 1583, though not by Gerard when he wrote about roses in England in the 1590s. In the middle of the next century it was reported to have been established in Norwich around the 1620s. There is no ground for believing the legend that it was linked to Henry II's mistress, Fair Rosamund, who died in 1176. Its present popularity in Britain is shown by the fact that it headed the table of Best Old Garden Roses in the Rose Analysis for 1995.

Viridiflora

VIRIDIFLORA GREEN ROSE, *R. CHINENSIS* VIRIDIFLORA

China bush

The so-called flowers are green, bronzing as they age, with narrow petals, especially in the centre where they take the place normally occupied by the stamens and the pistils. The blooms keep on appearing, sometimes in big clusters, from summer to late autumn, and though they are more of a curiosity than things of beauty, they certainly provide a talking point for visitors, and an odd item to include in flower arrangements. The plants grow bushy, to 75 x 60 cm (30 x 24 in), and leafy, with typical 'china' foliage, narrow, pointed and shiny.

This closely resembles an old Chinese garden rose, 'Lü E'. It was apparently growing in South Carolina about 1833 and was being offered by French growers in the 1850s, who received it from America via England.

Abraham Darby

MODERN SHRUB ROSES

ABRAHAM DARBY AUScot

Large-flowered shrub

The attraction of this rose is that it combines apricot-pink colour with old-style quartered blooms, a rare combination in shrub roses. The blooms are full of petals, large, 11 cm (4.5 in) across, have a fruity scent and hold a cupped shape as they open. The growth is strong up to 1.5 m (5 ft) tall and wide. The variety takes its name from a pioneer of Britain's Industrial Revolution who built the first iron bridge in 1777-79.
AUSTIN 1985.

BALLERINA

Polyantha shrub

This graceful plantsman's rose is one of the most notice-able of shrubs soon after midsummer, when its distinctive mophead clusters appear, closely packed with single light-pink blooms; at a distance the clusters could be taken for hydrangeas. They are carried close against a mass of small pointed leaflets on shrubby, dense, 1 x 1.2 m (40 x 48 in) plants.
BENTALL 1937.

BUFF BEAUTY

Cluster-flowered shrub

This belongs with what used to be called the hybrid musk roses, raised in the period 1913 onwards. Its large, light-apricot to buff flowers, full of short reflexing petals and pleasantly scented, are carried in big clusters on bowing stems. Seen against a background of handsome dark shiny foliage, they are one of summer's aesthetic pleasures in the garden; and there is more to come in autumn too. The plants grow shrubby and rounded to 1.2 m (4 ft) in height and width. This rose was introduced in 1939, and for years the identity of the raiser was uncertain. It is accepted now that the rose world should thank Ann Bentall.

Buff Beauty

Ballerina

CAREFREE WONDER MEIpitac

Cluster-flowered shrub

For a mass of colour this can be wonderfully effective, and useful as a hedge, in a bed or for a group in a mixed border. The colour is pink, with paler pink on the underside of the petals, giving a two-toned effect to the double flowers which hold a cupped shape as they open. They continue to bloom through summer and autumn, on free-branching, leafy bushes, 75 x 60 cm (30 x 24 in). This was an All America Rose Selection winner in its year of introduction.
MEILLAND 1991.

Carefree Wonder

Eyepaint

EYEPAINT TAPIS PERSAN, MACeye

Cluster-flowered shrub
(sometimes known as a cluster-flowered, or floribunda, bush rose)

This creates a dramatic effect as big clusters of scarlet buds open to show pale centres and yellow stamens. Growth is shrubby, 110 x 75 cm (42 x 30 in), with plentiful dark foliage sweeping to the ground. In milder climates, once established, it will often produce 2-3 m canes that some have mistaken for a climbing sport. The rose received Gold Medals in Baden-Baden and Belfast, and was bred from 'Picasso' by McGredy in 1975.
MCGREDY 1975.

FLOWER CARPET HEIDETRAUM, NOAtraum

Ground-cover shrub

Flower Carpet

Health is the big asset of this rose. In trials all over the UK its plentiful bright green leaves have shrugged off all attempts from neighbouring roses to worry them with fungus troubles. A pity the blooms are not more beautiful; they are deep rose pink, of middling size, carried in showy clusters for a long period in midsummer on spreading, bushy plants, 75 x 120 cm (30 x 48 in).
NOACK 1991.

FRANCINE AUSTIN AUSram

Cluster-flowered shrub

An unmistakable and beautiful variety, bearing dainty sprays of scented white pompom-type flowers on graceful arching stems, with distinctive long narrow leaves. This is one of the best shrub roses for a border where an informal type of plant is wanted, and it seems to be continually in bloom through the summer and autumn months. The plants grow to 90 x 120 cm (3 x 4 ft), and the parentage, a combination of noisette and polyantha shrub ('Alister Stella Gray' x 'Ballerina') is a reminder of how unconventional breeding can be rewarded with interesting results. AUSTIN 1988.

Francine Austin

Fru Dagmar Hastrup

FRU DAGMAR HASTRUP FRAU DAGMAR HARTOPP

Rugosa ground-cover shrub

The simple, wide-opening light-pink flowers, with their slightly ruffled petals and clove scent, are a favourite motif in schemes by landscape gardeners; they know their clients will appreciate a trouble-free shrub of modest size, blooming through the summer and bearing handsome hips in autumn. The hips are indeed among the best found among rugosa roses, resembling small tomatoes in their shape and colour. The wrinkled leathery leaves are also typical of Rugosa, providing good cover for most months of the year on spreading plants, 90 x 120 cm (3 x 4 ft).

For years two names, both awkward sounding, have been used for this rose. The Danish form is to be preferred to the German, since it acknowledges its country of origin.
HASTRUP 1914.

Golden Wings

GOLDEN WINGS

Shrub

Pale-yellow, single blooms open saucer-shaped, up to 12 cm (5 in) across, through summer and autumn. They look fragile against the tough, thorny shrubs that bear them, but this is deceptive, for they withstand bad weather well. They exude the sweet hay fragrance commonly found in Scots roses, one of which was used by rose historian Roy Shepherd in the breeding. The shrub is prickly and dense, to 1.1 x 1.3 m (42 x 54 in), and much favoured by gardeners who want roses with an informal look about them.
SHEPHERD 1956.

38

Graham Thomas

GRAHAM THOMAS AUSmas

Large-flowered shrub

Gardeners of two
centuries ago would
have rubbed their eyes and pinched themselves at the sight of this
rich yellow variety, with its big scented blooms quartered in the
style of the old garden roses, giving flower from summer to
autumn. No hardy full-petalled yellow rose existed then, and
autumn flowering was very limited.

The plant produces long arching stems, and becomes rather
open because the heavy flowers weigh down the branches. It will
cover 1.2 x 1.5 m (4 x 5 ft). Breeder David Austin introduced this
in 1983 and named it for the leading authority on old garden
roses.
AUSTIN 1983.

HERITAGE ROBERTA, AUSblush

Large-flowered shrub

There are over forty petals in the large blush-
pink flowers, which open cupped, with the
centre petals infolded. They have a refreshing
lemon fragrance, and maintain a good succession of bloom through summer and autumn.
The plant grows into a sturdy shrubby bush,
with a height and spread of 1.2 m (4 ft), with
plentiful dark foliage.
AUSTIN 1984.

Hertfordshire

HERTFORDSHIRE KORtenay

Ground-cover shrub

'Ground hugging' would be a fair description, for this rose keeps close to the soil at first, acquiring a humped appearance as new shoots grow over the old ones. The carpet of leaves thus provided is decorated with a fine succession of simple carmine-pink roses showing pale centres. They are borne in big clusters on short stems, nestling close against the foliage in a very attractive way. As a compact rose for the front of a border, to 45 x 90 cm (18 x 36 in), this rose is excellent, and its small bright leaves have a good health record.
KORDES 1991.

Heritage

Jacqueline Du Pré

JACQUELINE DU PRÉ   HARwanna

Cluster-flowered shrub

For a barrier hedge this has much to commend it. The plants are very vigorous, with prickly branching stems and excellent leaf cover, and the ivory to blush-white flowers appear by the end of May and do not stop coming until the autumn frosts. They are very noticeable, as they appear in clusters of several blooms together, each one 10 cm (4 in) across, with prominent reddish stamens; often they have scalloped petals, and there is a sweet scent. The growth can reach 1.5 x 1.2 m (60 x 54 in), or less if pruned hard. This rose was selected by the virtuoso 'cellist to bear her name, and received a Gold Medal in Le Roeulx.
HARKNESS 1989.

MANY HAPPY RETURNS   PRIMA, HARwanted

Cluster-flowered shrub
(sometimes known as a cluster-flowered, or floribunda, bush rose)

One might say 'many happy returns of the flower', because a bed or group of this seems never to be out of bloom from summer to late autumn. It bears clusters of slim buds which open into scented, cupped, semi-double pink flowers, 10 cm (4 in) across. The habit of growth is shrub-like and spreading, with dark shiny foliage, to 75 cm (30 in) high and wide.

The celebratory name actually derives from a railway company, who used the rose in a special promotion. It received a Gold Medal in Geneva in 1987.
HARKNESS 1991.

Many Happy Returns

MARGUERITE HILLING PINK NEVADA

Species hybrid

Marguerite Hilling

For spacious gardens, this distinctive rose will give a feast of beauty early in the summer, when the branches are garlanded with hundreds of 10 cm (4 in) blooms, in a warm and positive shade of pink. A few flowers appear later. The plants grow with strong arching stems to 2.2 m (7 ft) high and wide. The stems are dark and rather smooth, and when the main flush of flower has passed, their graceful bowing habit and clothing of light green leaves still form an attractive feature in the garden. This rose is a sport of 'Nevada', and was introduced by Hilling of Chobham, Surrey, in 1959.

MARTIN FROBISHER

Shrub rose

In many parts of Canada, the severe winters cause most roses to be frozen to ground level. Here is one bred by their Department of Agriculture for extra hardiness, using a rugosa strain. It bears blush to pink flowers, which open with the outer petals reflexing and the centre ones infolded. They are scented and continue to bloom through summer and autumn. The plants are rugged in appearance, with prickly stems and light green leaves, to 2 x 1.2 m (6 x 4 ft). Frobisher was an English navigator whose search for the Northwest Passage led him into the straits and bays of northern Canada in 1576-78.
SVEDJA 1968.

MARY ROSE AUSmary

Large-flowered shrub

The deep-rose-pink blooms are scented and have many petals, the outer ones reflexing while the inner ones curl inwards. This gives them a restful old-fashioned look. The plant has an uneven, shrubby habit, to 1.2 x 1 m (4 x 3 ft). It is named for the Mary Rose Trust, which worked to recover the remains of Henry VIII's flagship after it had lain on the seabed for 400 years.
AUSTIN 1983.

Mary Rose

Martin Frobisher

NOZOMI <small>HEIDEROSLEIN</small>

Ground-cover or miniature climber

The achievement of the breeder of this lowly rose, with its unassuming starry flowers, is remarkable. Ground-cover roses had been considered uninteresting and a waste of space. 'Nozomi', with its beauty and versatility, has now made them acceptable.

Masses of dainty blush to white flowers on trailing stems cover the plant in summer. 'Nozomi' is vigorous but lends itself to various uses, to edge pathways, to cover ground, to trail over walls, to grow in containers, to clamber over low structures and provide, in weeping standard form, a graceful centrepiece. The small leaflets, dark and bright, are attractive in themselves.

'Nozomi' is a Japanese name meaning 'hope', and commemorates the daughter of Canon Imai of the Canadian Anglican Church. She died in tragic circumstances when only four years old. Her uncle, the breeder Dr Toru Onodera, named his rose for her. It was introduced in 1968.
ONODERA 1968.

Nozomi

Octavia Hill

OCTAVIA HILL   HARzeal

Large-flowered shrub rose

This combines the beauty of many nineteenth-century roses, cherished for their rounded form and quartered centres, with the repeat-flowering character and handsome foliage of modern ones. The scented flowers are sizeable, light pink, deepening in colour towards the middle, and borne on bowing stems. They contrast well with the dark foliage. The plants grow with a neat shrubby habit to 1.2 x 1 m (4 x 3 ft). Octavia Hill was one of the founders of The National Trust in England and the rose is named to mark its Centenary.
HARKNESS 1995.

PEARL DRIFT LEGgab

Cluster-flowered shrub

This is a rose to rest the eyes. The gentle blush colour of the blooms accords well with the dark leaves and graceful rounded outline of the plant. The flowers are scented, appear in wide clusters and open, saucer-like, to 10 cm (4 in) across. For a neat-growing shrub in a bed or border to give many flowers through the season, it is a good choice. Grows to 1 x 1.2 m (3 x 4 ft). The parentage shows that the raiser got seed out of the usually sterile 'Mermaid', which he had pollinated with 'New Dawn'. LEGRICE 1980.

Pearl Drift

PENELOPE

Cluster-flowered shrub

The scented, shell-pink flowers are beautifully formed, cupped at first, then opening to display gold stamens. It is a great old favourite, well foliaged and easy to place in the company of roses of any period, in a border, or to grow as a hedge. At peak flowering time in summer, the big flower clusters almost hide the 1 x 1 m (40 x 40 in) plants. There is another good display in autumn. The National Rose Society awarded this rose its Gold Medal in 1925, the year following its introduction by the clergyman-turned-nurseryman, the Rev. Joseph Pemberton.

Penelope

Pink Grootendorst

PINK GROOTENDORST

Rugosa shrub

The point of growing this variety is to enjoy the curious rose-pink flowers, which have tiny serrations along the petal edges. There are white and red forms, and all of them form tough, upright, rather open shrubs, with leathery leaves and prickly stems, to 1.3 x 1.1 m (54 x 42 in).
GROOTENDORST 1923.

Roseraie de l'Haÿ

ROSERAIE DE L'HAŸ

Rugosa shrub

The colour impact of this rose is considerable, because the rich purple-red blooms are sizeable – 11 cm (4.5 in) across – and appear in quantity in summer, with good continuity until autumn. They are full petalled, open out flat with yellow stamens showing, have tremendous fragrance and look magnificent against handsomely foliaged, rounded 2 m (6 ft) shrubs. The leaves are of rugosa type, leathery, wrinkled and deep bright green. If you can stand the colour and have the space, this is one of the best of all garden roses – hardy, weather proof, trouble free, and with leaves that persist well into the winter.
COCHET-COCHET 1901.

ROSY CUSHION INTERALL

Cluster-flowered shrub

Rosy Cushion

The sweetly scented flowers are pink with ivory hearts, opening like shallow saucers in big clusters. As its name leads you to expect, the rose has a spreading habit to 1 x 1.2 m (3 x 4 ft), with plentiful dark shiny foliage. It is more of a shrub rose than a ground-cover rose, in which guise it is often sold. It is excellent in a mixed flower border.
ILSINK 1979.

Sally Holmes

SALLY HOLMES

Cluster-flowered shrub

The character of this rose can best be appreciated in warm climates, where the inflorescence is extended after the manner of a delphinium spike; leaving one to ponder what future surprises the rose genes have in store.

It is a beautiful variety, forming great heads of buff-white to ivory blooms in spectacular clusters on tall stems. The growth is upright and narrow to 2 x 1m (6 x 3 ft), with large, dark glossy leaves. There is some scent and it is popular with exhibitors. Raised and named by R. A. Holmes of Cheshire, and introduced in 1976.

HOLMES 1976.

SURREY SOMMERWIND, VENT D'ÉTÉ, KORlanum

Ground-cover shrub

The picture shows the rose grown as a standard in the Peace Memorial Park, Itami, Japan. This is a vigorous rose, and as a shrub is will make a leafy mound and decorate it with a good quantity of bloom for many weeks in summer to autumn. The flowers are rose pink, lightly scented, of rounded form, with twenty or so ruffled petals, borne in clusters along the stems. The growth is spreading, shrubby, to 80 x 120 cm (32 x 48 in), well covered with dark leaves. It scored well for novelty and health in its trials, winning Gold Medals and other major prizes. KORDES 1985.

Surrey

The Fairy

THE FAIRY

Polyantha shrub
(sometimes known as a cluster-flowered, or floribunda, bush rose or a patio bush rose)

The dainty sprays of this little rose, with their rosettes of clear rose pink, are always a delight. It is one of the later roses to come on flower, but then continues until the frosts of winter. The habit of growth is cushiony, to a height and spread of 60 cm (2 ft), or more if it is left unpruned or grown against a wall. As a standard it is most effective, creating an 'umbrella' head with masses of petite shiny leaves. It has always been hard to classify, because there is nothing else quite like it; if it were a novelty today it might be considered a patio ground-cover rose.
BENTALL 1932.

Tigris

TIGRIS HARprier

Persica hybrid shrub

Rosa persica grows in southwest Asia with stems and leaves unlike those of any other rose, and a distinctive scarlet eye at the base of its canary yellow petals. 'Tigris' is one of a few varieties successfully bred from it. The blooms are small and fairly full of petals, each one having red at the base. It flowers quite freely in summer on wiry stems, and forms a prickly spreading mound, 45 x 60 cm (18 x 24 in). The leaves are variable, as if undecided whether to behave conventionally or not.
HARKNESS 1985

WESTERLAND KORwest

Cluster-flowered shrub

After several years in commerce, this rose is becoming popular, not by reason of undue publicity, but because its excellent garden qualities are at last being recognised. The colour is rare among shrub roses, apricot-orange with some yellow, taking salmon tones as the flowers age. The blooms are fragrant and have waved, rather short petals, giving an air of informality as they open to admit the stamens to view; and they keep coming from summer to autumn. Growth is sturdy, upright, to 2 x 1.2 m (6 x 4 ft), and the plants are handsomely clothed in bright green leaves.

Westerland

CLIMBING AND RAMBLING ROSES, OLD AND NEW

ALBÉRIC BARBIER

Rambler

Petite creamy-yellow buds opening into creamy-white flowers provide a beautiful picture in early to midsummer. They are carried very freely against a mass of small, dark, glossy leaflets. The blooms are about 8 cm (3 in) across and well filled with narrow quilled petals. The stems are long, supple, easy to train, and effective for concealing any kind of structure for nine months of the year, since the leaves persist well into winter. Growth is rambling, 5 x 4 m (15 x 12 ft). BARBIER 1900.

Albéric Barbier

Albertine

ALBERTINE

Rambler

This is the sort of variety that comes to mind when we picture
the ideal cottage garden. A wealth of fragrant light-rosy-salmon
blooms of regular form nestle among red-stemmed branches at all
levels of the plant – but only for one glorious month of summer. It
makes vigorous, indeed rampant, growth, up to 5 x 4 m (15 x
12 ft) and is best used where space allows it to grow naturally,
with unproductive wood removed every third year or so. It is often
planted inadvisedly against walls, where mildew may be trouble-
some.
BARBIER 1921.

Alister Stella Gray

ALISTER STELLA GRAY GOLDEN RAMBLER

Noisette climber

This is a great favourite with lovers of the older roses, with its graceful clusters of numerous pale yellow blooms with confused yolk-yellow centres; they whiten as they age, have refreshing scent and provide some good-quality late-season bloom. The weight of the flower clusters causes the long slender stems to arch down gracefully, and the plants need space, for they can reach 4.5 x 3 m (15 x 10 ft), or more in mild climates. A high wall free of frost suits best.
GRAY 1894.

Aloha

ALOHA

Large-flowered climber
sometimes listed as a shrub rose

Grown on a wall, this makes a climber up to 3 x 2.5 m (10 x 8 ft) laden with full-petalled rose and salmon-pink blooms, of exquisite old style quartered form and with good fragrance. It can be kept pruned and grown as a stalwart, rather uneven shrub. There is a good succession of bloom through summer and autumn, and the large, dark leaves form a good background to the 9 cm (3.5 in) blooms.
BOERNER 1949.

ALTISSIMO DELmur

Climber

Seven big petals in deep bright red open to reveal golden-yellow stamens, a beautiful sight from summer to late autumn. The flowers come both one to a stem and in clusters, and they are large (12 cm, 5 in) across. So this rose can claim to be large-flowered and cluster-flowered, causing a puzzle for obsessive classifiers of rose groups. The growth is strong and stiff to 3 x 2.5 m (10 x 8 ft), with dark foliage.
DELBARD-CHABERT 1966.

Altissimo

AMERICAN PILLAR

Climber

One of the most noticeable roses in midsummer, when its arching stems are a mass of little five-petalled flowers, each with a white eye in the centre of its carmine petals. The display lasts three to four weeks, after which some of the oldest flowering stems can be taken out to make room for vigorous new shoots. The plant makes rampant growth to 4 x 3 m (12 x 10 ft) and has tough glossy foliage, occasionally dulled by mildew.
VAN FLEET 1902.

American Pillar

Breath of Life

BREATH OF LIFE HARquanne

Large-flowered hybrid tea climber

People love this rose for its rare colour, apricot to apricot-pink. The blooms are large, of full-petalled hybrid tea form, pleasantly scented and excellent for cutting; they last as well as any rose, opening slowly and changing their colour tone in a fascinating way. If you want an all-purpose trouble-free climber of upright growth for pillar, wall or fence, this is a good one (though it is difficult to find in the US). The flowers appear through summer and autumn. Grows 3 x 2 m (10 x 6 ft), or less if trimmed as a tall shrub. Requires winter protection in harsh climates.

The name was chosen by The Royal College of Midwives in London as the result of a naming competition, to mark their Centenary year.
HARKNESS 1982.

CHAMPNEYS' PINK CLUSTER

Noisette climber

This is an important variety in rose history, and a fine garden plant for mild climates, or in a sheltered site. It bears scented, prettily formed, cupped, double pink flowers, about 5 cm (2 in) across, in summer. The stems are rather smooth, and carry attractive shiny foliage. In favourable conditions this rose is capable of attaining 2.5 to 4 m in height (8–12 ft) and 2.5 m (8 ft) in width.
CHAMPNEYS 1811.

Champneys'
Pink Cluster

CITY GIRL HARzorba

Climbing or shrub rose

City Girl

The cupped, semi-double flowers of this rose are a cheerful shade of salmon pink, with good fragrance. They appear in large clusters from summer to autumn, and open wide to 11 cm (4.5 in) across, showing a warm expanse of colour. Growth is vigorous, with a good cover of dark glossy foliage, to 2.2 m (7 ft) tall and wide; the plant can be pruned to maintain a shorter, shrubby habit if desired. The name commemorates the centenary of The City of London School for Girls.
HARKNESS 1994.

COMPASSION BELLE DE LONDRES

Large-flowered hybrid tea climber

A great favourite because it has delicious fragrance, large flowers of pretty form, handsome dark leaves and the ability to bloom freely throughout summer and autumn. The colour is light rosy salmon, with apricot tints as you look into the flower. It is moreover an obliging plant; you can prune it hard to form a vigorous shrub, or train it to 3 x 2.5 m (10 x 8 ft) on wall, fence or pillar.
HARKNESS 1973.

Compassion

Crimson Shower

CRIMSON SHOWER

Rambler

This rose is astonishing because of its blooming period. In England, it starts in late July when other ramblers have finished, and dense clusters of crimson rosettes are maintained right through August into September. The stems carry hundreds of tiny polished leaflets, and growth is vigorous but lax, so it needs a good support to reach 2.5 x 2.2 m (8 x 7 ft).
NORMAN 1951.

DORTMUND

Climber or shrub

If you want a rose constantly in bloom, with eye-catching qualities and excellent health, this is hard to equal. It produces many clusters which nestle against the foliage, full of deep red flowers which open to reveal whitish eyes. The leaves – dark and glossy – form a handsome background. The growth is upright, 3 x 1.8 m (10 x 6 ft) when supported, or less if pruned and grown as a shrub. This is one of the famous line of hardy varieties, raised from *R. kordesii* by Wilhelm Kordes, and was introduced in 1955.
KORDES 1955.

Dortmund

ENA HARKNESS, CLIMBING

Hybrid tea climber

After the Second World War the bush form of this rose became the most popular red rose, by reason of its rich bright crimson colour, high-centred blooms and prettily furled petals. Add to that a fragrance strong enough to win prizes, and the faults – frail flower stems and skimpy leaf cover – were excused for many years. Today the climbing version is well worth growing, since nodding stems are advantageous at eye level and above. It makes stiff, branching growth to 4.5 x 2.5 m (15 x 8 ft). A family friend, Albert Norman, raised the bush form and wanted to name it for rose grower Bill Harkness, but Bill suggested it bear his wife's name instead. It appeared in 1946, and the climbing sport followed in 1954 from two different sources, R. Murrell in Hertfordshire and Gurteen & Ritson in Surrey. Only very limited availability in the US.

Ena Harkness, climbing

FÉLICITÉ-PERPÉTUE   FÉLICITÉ ET PERPÉTUE

Climber

The flowers are charming, formed by row upon row of tiny white petals, often tipped red in the bud stage. During late summer the clusters are so prolific that they seem to cascade down whatever structure the plant is trained on, and it is a good coverer of eyesores, making vigorous growth in all directions up to 5 x 4 m (15 x 12 ft), and with plenty of narrow dark leaves.

This is one of several climbers raised by the gardener to the Duc d'Orléans (later King Louis Philippe), A. Jacques, using *R. sempervirens*, the 'evergreen' species rose. He is said to have intended to name the variety after an expected arrival in the family; when twin girls were born, their names were conjoined, no doubt with conscious reference to the early Christian martyrs who perished together in AD 203. The rose was introduced in 1827 and is the only rose in commerce named for two individuals.

Félicité-Perpétue

GLOIRE DE DIJON   OLD GLORY ROSE

Noisette climber

'Glory John' is another version of the name, reflecting the inability of English gardeners to cope with the Gallic tongue. This

Gloire de Dijon

rose is famous the world over for its pretty buff-yellow flowers, opening quartered, with pleasing scent, and its success has been further assured by its vigour, capable of covering 5 x 4 m (15 x 12 ft) or more; in *The Rose* magazine for Christmas 1992, a specimen was recorded of 5 x 8 m (16 x 24 ft) which was having to be restrained from extending further. It looks best on a wall where the stiff branches can be trained firmly in place. The parentage is supposedly a tea rose crossed with the Bourbon 'Souvenir de la Malmaison'. It is still a popular rose today, and a reminder of the pre-eminence of French breeders in the nineteenth century.
JACOTOT 1853.

GOLDEN SHOWERS

Climber or shrub rose

The cheerful bright yellow flowers appear constantly from summer to autumn, opening out wide from long slim buds to give a colourful show. This, together with the sweet fragrance and the plant's general good health and bright foliage, are reasons for its continuing popularity after so many years in commerce. The habit is upright, and it can look spindly if not trained sideways when grown on a wall or fence. It will cover 3 x 2 m (10 x 6 ft) or can be pruned to form a 2 m (6 ft) shrub. It won the Portland Gold Medal, awarded for roses of proven performance, in 1957.
LAMMERTS 1957

Golden Showers

HANDEL MACha

Climber

The blush flowers with their red rims and neat form are seen often, for this is one of the most photogenic of all roses, and as the period of flower extends through summer to autumn, flowers are often on hand for the camera. They contrast well with dark foliage on plants of upright stiff growth, to 3 x 2.2 m (10 x 7 ft). The Portland Gold Medal, awarded to roses of proven good performance, was bestowed on 'Handel' in 1975.
MCGREDY 1965.

High Hopes

HIGH HOPES HARyup

Climber

There are many pink climbers, and this one scores well for vigour, for freedom of flower over a long period, and for the pretty form of its scented light-pink blooms. The buds are slim and elegant, just right for buttonholes. The foliage is plentiful and very dark green, which makes it a good foil for the pale flowers. For covering up walls, fences and trellis this is an effective plant, reaching 3 x 2.2 m (10 x 7 ft) or more. It won the Gold Medal in the 1992 Japanese Rose Trials.
HARKNESS 1992.

68

Lady Hillingdon, climbing

LADY HILLINGDON, CLIMBING

Tea climber

The long slender buds of this light apricot-yellow rose have been seen in gardens since 1910, but the bush that bore them was frail and spindly. Seven years later an English nurseryman introduced a vigorous climbing sport, and this is the form usually seen today. The growth is stiff and free branching to 5 x 2.5 m (15 x 8 ft), with unusual purple foliage. It gives the best results in a sheltered site, because, like all pure tea roses, it is of limited hardiness. ELISHA HICKS 1917.

MAIGOLD

Climber

When bare of flower this is an unappealing rose, with stiffly branching stems and many prickles. In early summer there is a transformation. The same stems are wreathed in scented, bronzy-yellow flowers, opening wide to display the stamens and enjoy early attention from the bees. There are intermittent blooms later in the season.

The leaves are tough and leathery, the whole plant very hardy (being bred from a Scots rose line) and likely to attain a height and spread of 2.5 m (8 ft) or more. KORDES 1953.

Maigold

MERMAID

Climber

Mermaid

'Awkward on land' has been said of this rose, referring to the time it takes to get established, and also to the brittle nature of the shoots which may break if bent too far in training. Yellow flowers with five big petals open to 11 cm (4.5 in) across, the colour fading to cream before the petals furl back and drop, leaving a ring of amber stamens. The flowering period extends from midsummer, or earlier in sheltered sites, until late autumn. The growth is stiff and free branching, up to 6 x 6 m (20 x 20 ft), with distinctive shiny leaves, tinted red when young, and hooked prickles. 'Mermaid' is a good wall climber, though sites exposed to windborne frost should be avoided; it looks best where it is growing naturally, free to romp around. R. bracteata and a tea rose were the parents of this remarkable variety, which rarely sets any seed. It received a Gold Medal from the National Rose Society in 1917.

W. PAUL & SON 1918.

MME ALFRED CARRIÈRE

Noisette climber

The apparent frailty of the young shoots on this rose is belied by its survival and continuing popularity, after over a century in commerce. In its favour are the pretty, loosely formed gardenia-like flowers, white with a hint of blush, and scented; extended period of flower from summer to autumn; and vigour, enabling it to achieve 6 x 3 m (18 x 10 ft). Seasonal mildew is only a passing inconvenience. The variety was introduced in 1879 by the Schwartz nursery in south-east France, and named for a local rose lover.

Mme Alfred Carrière

MME GRÉGOIRE STAECHELIN   SPANISH BEAUTY

Climber

Mme Grégoire Staechelin

Many roses are hard to identify at first glance, but there is no mistaking the flowers of this one, with their rosy-pink waved petals, randomly streaked with crimson, opening out to flaunt their beauty on vigorous branching plants; especially when these flowers seem to cover most of the plant, and appear earlier than most other roses. The rose does not give any later bloom, forming sizeable hips instead, which should be trimmed off if you can get at them. This can be difficult since the plant makes tremendous growth, capable of reaching 6 x 4 m (20 x 12 ft). Introduced by Dot of Spain in 1927, the year it won first prize in the trials at Bagatelle in Paris.
DOT 1927.

Morning Jewel

MORNING JEWEL

Climber

This is well named, for the bright pink flowers seen against handsome glossy foliage have a brilliant, jewel-like quality, especially when caught by the morning sun. The summer flowering is spectacular, and incidental blooms appear later until the autumn; they have a pleasing fragrance. The growth is stiff, free branching, with healthy foliage to 4 x 2.5 m (12 x 8 ft), and this is a good item to try on a 'difficult' wall site.
COCKER 1968.

NEW DAWN EVERBLOOMING DR VAN FLEET

Climber or shrub

Few roses can have given as much pleasure as 'New Dawn'. Sprays of pretty blush flowers open whatever the weather, they have sweet fragrance, the leaves are handsome and plentiful and blooming continues right through from summer until curtailed by autumn frosts. It is also most adaptable, making a tough hedge if pruned hard, or easily trained over pillars, fences and garden walls to 3 x 2.5 m (10 x 8 ft).

Introduced by Somerset Rose Nurseries of the US in 1930, it was the first rose in the world to enjoy the protection of a Plant Patent.

New Dawn

Parkdirektor Riggers

PARKDIREKTOR RIGGERS

Climber

Despite the awkward name, this is a popular rose for its bright, deep-red, stiff-petalled flowers, borne in trusses of as many as fifty blooms. Other assets are its hardiness, vigour and ability to give a colourful display through summer and autumn. The growth is stiff, strongly branching, 4 x 2.5 m (12 x 8 ft). Bred by Kordes 1957, with *R. kordesii* in the parentage.
KORDES 1957.

RAMBLING RECTOR

Rambler

This is another rose that, like 'Kiftsgate', can be a horticultural disaster in the wrong place. It makes a rampageous, arching 6 x 6 m (20 x 20 ft) scrambler, ideal for growing into trees or putting on an extensive pergola or setting free in a wild garden. A plant in full flower resembles a creamy-white cloud, with innumerable clusters of small, semi-double flowers. A fine specimen at St Albans is intertwined with a tall conifer, and accords well with Graham Thomas's terse comment, 'impenetrable, un-prunable, overpowering'.

Its origin is unknown; *R. multiflora* probably comes into it, and it was being grown before 1912.

Rambling Rector

Rosa banksiae lutea

RAMONA RED CHEROKEE

Climber

Ramona

The flowers of this unusual rose are carmine red, with a greyish-red reverse and gold stamens. They display their five petals to good effect, opening 10 cm (4 in) across, and the sight is the more welcome because it comes early in the season before most other roses. The growth is stiff and open to 2.5 x 3 m (8 x 10 ft) and the foliage is sparse.

The Cherokee rose is another name for *R. laevigata*, a beautiful Chinese wild rose with long silky petals and gold stamens, which is too tender to grow in frost-prone areas. From it, probably crossed with a tea rose, came *R. x anemonoides* in 1895, and 'Ramona' is a sport of that, introduced by Dietrich & Turner of California in 1913. In cooler climates it needs a warm wall to do well.
DIETRICH & TURNER 1913.

ROSA BANKSIAE LUTEA BANKSIAN YELLOW

Wild climbing rose

Graceful' is the word for this eye-catching and unmistakable yellow rose, bearing dainty clusters of small-petalled flowers in early summer. They cover plants that can extend 5 x 2.5 m (15 x 8 ft) or more. The leaves are light green, smooth and narrow, and the bark surface on old stems flakes away in layers. All in all a fascinating rose to grow, but it needs a site where frost cannot affect it. It is named for the wife of the eminent botanist and explorer Sir Joseph Banks (1742-1820), and was brought from its native China to London in 1824.

ROSA MULLIGANII

Wild climbing rose

Hundreds of pendant stems laden with clusters of white flowers create an unforgettable picture of beauty as you view a pergola planted with this rose. The period of bloom is fleeting, but worth the wait. The growth is strong and clambering to 5 x 3 m (15 x 10 ft), and it has handsome, large shiny leaves.

The curious fact is that no one seems very sure of the true identity of the rose offered by growers under this name, seed of which was sent from Yunnan to the RHS Gardens at Wisley in 1919. Plants supplied as *R. longicuspis* are often found to be the same. The identity of Bryan Mulligan is surer; he was the Assistant to the Director at Wisley. The botanist to whom he sent the specimens to be identified named the rose after him.

Rosa mulliganii

LARGE-FLOWERED (HYBRID TEA) BUSH ROSES

Alexander

ALEXANDER ALEXANDRA, HARlex

Large-flowered hybrid tea bush

It might be fairer to call this a shrub, because it can reach 2 x 1 m (6 x 3 ft) easily, bearing eye-catching vermilion-red blooms on long stiff stems. The blooms are double, 12 cm (5 in) across, often with scalloped petals. However, size will diminish where hot nights prevail. The vigour, good health and attractive shiny leaves of this rose have earned it many prizes, including the James Mason Medal for the rose that has given special pleasure over the past fifteen years, awarded in 1987. Two of the biggest plants of 'Alexander' ever seen flank the grave of Field Marshal the Earl Alexander of Tunis in whose honour it is named, at Ridge in Hertfordshire.
HARKNESS 1972.

Brigadoon

Big Purple

BIG PURPLE NUIT D'ORIENT, STEPHENS' BIG PURPLE, STEbigpu

Large-flowered hybrid tea bush

Size, colour and scent are the great assets of this rose. The blooms are well formed, 12 cm (5 in) across, of a rich beetroot-purple colour, carried boldly on strong stems and with powerful sweet fragrance. They flower from summer to autumn, and are excellent for cutting. The plants grow with a stiff, rather arching habit to 90 x 60 cm (36 x 24 in) and carry large dark leaves. STEPHENS 1987.

BRIGADOON JACpal

Large-flowered hybrid tea bush

The lovely colour of this rose is a combination of blush at the centre and strawberry red towards the petal edges, the reddish tones becoming more pronounced in the later stages. The full-petalled 12 cm (5 in) blooms have high centres, and their pretty spiral form makes them attractive to cut for the house from summer to autumn. The plants grow bushily to 100 x 70 cm (36 x 28 in), and their overall merits were recognised by an All America Rose Selection award in 1992.
WARRINER 1991.

DAINTY BESS

Large-flowered hybrid tea bush

It was an accepted practice in 1925 to call a five-petalled rose measuring 9 cm (3.5 in) across a hybrid tea. We would not so regard it today. 'Dainty Bess' has proved a great survivor, and the pretty pale-pink flowers with noticeable maroon stamens still delight gardeners the world over. The leaves are dark, and growth bushy, to 75 x 60 cm (30 x 24 in). It received the National Rose Society's Gold Medal in 1925.
ARCHER 1925.

Dainty Bess

Die Welt

Double Delight

DIE WELT THE WORLD, DIEKOR

Large-flowered hybrid tea bush

There is no doubt about the large-flower quality of this reddish-orange and yellow rose. The blooms can measure 10 cm (5 in) across and its wide petals make it ideal for showing. It is not free flowering enough as a garden rose and it seems to have a bout of mildew each autumn. Growth is upright, 80 x 60 cm (32 x 24 in). KORDES 1976.

DOUBLE DELIGHT

Large-flowered hybrid tea bush

One expects a lot of a rose that was voted the World's Favourite in 1985, and holds Gold Medals and fragrance prizes too. The colour blend – blush pink edged and flushed carmine – is indeed a 'delight', as is the scent. In warm seasons it is wonderful, with big blooms of perfect high-centred form produced in surprising abundance. Less desirable is its performance in cold wet weather, when the flowers often ball up. The growth is branching and uneven to 90 x 75 cm (36 x 24 in).
SWIM & ELLIS 1977.

Elina

ELINA   PEAUDOUCE, DICjana

Large-flowered hybrid tea bush

There is much to admire in this variety. The huge shapely flowers are scented and have big wide petals of ivory with lemon at their base, thus enlivening the centre of the blooms. The leaves provide a perfect contrast, being dark green and so plentiful that they clothe the bush almost to the ground. They may be touched by mildew but it soon clears up. Growth is upright and vigorous to 1.1 m x 75 cm (42 x 30 in). 'Elina' is a major prizewinner in Germany, New Zealand, the US and the UK, where it gained the James Mason prize in 1995.
DICKSON 1985.

Fragrant Cloud

FRAGRANT CLOUD DUFTWOLKE, NUAGE PARFUMÉ, TANellis

Large-flowered hybrid tea bush

Surely one of the best named roses ever; the scent is as strong as anyone could wish for. Large, dusky scarlet blooms appear through summer and autumn with great freedom, considering their size, on strong large-leaved plants. The growth is bushy to 75 x 60 cm (30 x 24 in). Winner of the top St Albans award and the coveted Portland Gold Medal.
TANTAU 1963.

Freedom

FREEDOM DICjem

Large-flowered hybrid tea bush

A bed of this rose makes a glorious sight, because it grows evenly, is handsomely foliaged, and the rich bright yellow of the flowers stands out to great effect. At 9 cm (3.5 in) across, the blooms are on the small side, and that is no doubt why the plants are able to produce them so freely through summer and autumn. Because the bloom size diminishes in hot weather, this rose never made it onto the US market. The habit is bushy and vigorous to 75 x 60 cm (30 x 24 in). The rose's merits have been recognised by Gold Medals at St Albans and The Hague.
DICKSON 1984.

Fyvie Castle

FYVIE CASTLE AMBERLIGHT, COCbamber

Large-flowered hybrid tea bush

A rose whose wide petals and big rounded flowers, up to 13 cm (5.5 in) across, make it well suited to warmer climates. The colour is variable, a blend of amber with apricot-pink tints, and there is a pleasing fragrance. As a bedding rose this is a good choice, with a neat, bushy habit, 60 cm (2 ft) tall and wide.

Fyvie Castle is in the care of the National Trust for Scotland. The name 'Amberlight' was preferred for use in New Zealand, where the rose won the premier trials award.
COCKER 1985.

Gold Medal

GOLD MEDAL AROYQUELI

Large-flowered hybrid tea bush

In a warm climate this is one of the best yellow garden roses, free flowering and producing high-centred, well proportioned flowers on firm stems. Sometimes they are borne singly, sometimes in a cluster, and there is a pleasing fruity fragrance. The colour is liable to fade in hot sun, and though it is very popular in the US and New Zealand (where it won the Gold Medal that inspired the name), it does not suit cooler climates.
CHRISTENSEN 1982.

Ingrid Bergman

INGRID BERGMAN   POULMAN

Large-flowered hybrid tea bush

This produces some of the loveliest dark-red roses seen today, with long petals and classic high-centred form. They are carried on strong stems bearing large, shiny, leathery leaves. The plants are upright, somewhat uneven in habit, to 80 x 65 cm (32 x 26 in). The Golden Rose of The Hague award, together with Gold Medals in Belfast and Madrid, bear witness both to its good qualities and to its acceptability for different climates. POULSEN 1984.

JUST JOEY

Large-flowered hybrid tea bush

A distinctive rose for its rare copper-buff colour, very large flowers and prettily frilled petals. It caused a sensation when first exhibited, and has proved its worth by achieving two of the most prestigious awards - the James Mason Memorial Medal as a rose that has given special pleasure over a period of years (in 1986) and the title of The World's Favourite Rose in 1994. There is some scent too, enough to earn it a prize at The Hague.

The leaves are dark and handsome, though not as plentiful as one could wish. Feed this rose well, and you will be rewarded with some of the loveliest blooms you will see anywhere, perfect to cut for the house. It received its name as the result of a mis-heard conversation. The raiser thought of naming it for his wife, Joey Pawsey, but that seemed something of a tongue twister. 'Why not call it just "Joey"', said his father – and 'Just Joey' it became. CANT 1974.

Just Joey

LOVING MEMORY BURGUND 81, RED CEDAR, KORgund

Large-flowered hybrid tea bush

Some years ago the search was on for a rose with a suitable name for planting in British crematoriums. Out of several candidates this dark red was chosen. It has very large flowers, 12 cm (5 in) across, carried high on strong plants, and, considering the size of bloom, flowers extremely well through summer and autumn. It grows upright and vigorously to 110 x 75 cm (42 x 30 in). KORDES 1981.

Loving Memory

MARY-JEAN HARyen

Large-flowered hybrid tea bush

Mary-Jean

The colour is amber-apricot, deepening at the centre, thus giving a delightful depth to the flower. With over forty wide petals, the 12 cm (5 in) blooms are among the largest of the hybrid teas, and at their best - and most fragrant - in warm weather. The plants are well foliaged with dark leaves and grow bushily to 90 x 70 cm (36 x 28 in). Mary-Jean was the wife of Peter Green of Bermuda, who named the rose as a token of his love for her. HARKNESS 1991.

NEW ZEALAND AOTEAROA, MACgnev

Large-flowered hybrid tea bush

The light-salmon-pink flowers have lovely form and good size – 12 cm (5 in) across - but the main asset of this variety is its fragrance, sweet and strong. There is a tendency for flower stems to nod under the heavy blooms. The plants grow bushy, well clothed with glossy foliage, to 80 x 60 cm (32 x 24 in). 'Aotearoa' is the Maori name for New Zealand, and is usually translated as 'the land of the long white cloud'.
MCGREDY 1990.

New Zealand

Pascali

PASCALI LENIP

Large-flowered hybrid tea bush

This is the latest addition to the Hall of Fame, made up of roses that have won the triennial contest for The World's Favourite Rose. The milk-white blooms are always perfectly formed, with high centres, and excellent to cut. They are produced very freely, on upright plants that could do with more foliage cover, growing to 75 x 50 cm (30 x 20 in). The name 'Pascali' means Easter, the festival when white is the liturgical colour, symbolising purity.
LENS 1963.

Paul Shirville

PAUL SHIRVILLE   HEART THROB, SAXO, HARqueterwife

Large-flowered hybrid tea bush

A photographer described this as 'the most photogenic rose I know', and certainly the fragrant, rosy salmon-pink flowers have classic hybrid tea form, with furled petals holding a true centre while the outer petals reflex to form a circular outline. In its general effect the plant may be considered a hybrid tea shrub, as these blooms are carried at different levels on the spreading, shrubby plant, 80 x 75 cm (32 x 30 in). There is a generous cover of dark foliage.

The rose was named as a retirement surprise present, and the recipient is perhaps the only individual who has a credit card (from a Scottish bank) depicting 'his' rose. It holds fragrance awards in England and New Zealand.
HARKNESS 1983.

90

Peace

PEACE GIOIA, GLORIA DEI, MME A. MEILLAND

Large-flowered hybrid tea bush

If there is a 'rose of the century', surely this is it. 'Peace' set new standards for other varieties to follow, because it has so many virtues: beautiful form, good petal texture, indifference to weather and to climate, vigour, foliage cover and hardiness. Its beguiling yellow-flushed-pink blooms were named by the raiser for his mother, but it was used as decoration at the postwar Peace Conference in the US, and there was no going back on the name 'Peace' after that. The growth is shrubby and strong to 120 x 90 cm (4 x 3 ft). Its four Gold Medals include The Golden Rose of The Hague. MEILLAND 1942.

Rosemary Harkness

Renaissance

RENAISSANCE HARzart

Large-flowered hybrid tea bush

At their best, the pearly white roses with their refreshing fragrance and perfect form are among the loveliest roses you will find. This was raised by crossing 'Amber Queen' with 'Margaret Merril', and combines their leafiness, vigour, freedom of bloom, and also the scent; it received the Fragrance Prize in Belfast in 1995. The habit is bushy, 75 x 65 cm (30 x 26 in). It was named for NADFAS, The National Association of Decorative and Fine Art Societies.
HARKNESS 1994.

ROSEMARY HARKNESS HARrowbond

Large-flowered hybrid tea bush

Sweet scent, pretty form and a cheerful mix of colours make this a desirable garden rose. The long buds are peachy-orange, showing apricot-yellow and salmon-pink tones as the petals unfold. The growth is shrubby, uneven, averaging 80 cm (32 in) tall and wide, and the dark glossy leaves have attractive reddish tints when young. This holds fragrance awards from Glasgow and from Belfast, where it also received the Gold Medal. It is named for Peter Harkness's younger daughter to mark her coming of age. Limited availability in the US.
HARKNESS 1985.

Royal William

Savoy Hotel

ROYAL WILLIAM DUFTZAUBER 84, FRAGRANT CHARM 84, KORzaun

Large-flowered hybrid tea bush

For a robust garden rose, giving a succession of fragrant, deep crimson blooms on long cuttable stems from summer to autumn, this is an excellent choice. The high-centred flowers, 12 cm (5 in) across, are large enough for exhibition, and they hold their colour well. The growth is upright and vigorous to 100 x 75 cm (36 x 30 in), with plentiful large dark leaves. It was named to mark King William III's coming to England in 1688, and was voted Rose of the Year by British growers.
KORDES 1984.

SAVOY HOTEL INTEGRITY, VERCORS, HARvintage

Large-flowered hybrid tea bush

Light pink, but surprisingly vibrant for such a subtle shade, due to the deeper pink tones on the petal reverse; as the flowers open, these attract the eye and give depth and interest to the blooms. They are large and freely produced on strong, well branched bushes, good for bedding, 80 x 60 cm (32 x 24 in), with dark leaves. This received a Gold Medal in Dublin.
HARKNESS 1989.

SILVER JUBILEE

Large-flowered hybrid tea bush

This might be thought too well known to need description, but in fact it does not do well in warmer countries so is little seen there. The rosy-salmon and peach-pink blooms open from buds of average size into surprisingly large flowers, maintaining, with their high centres and symmetry of form, the very best traditions of the hybrid tea roses. The plants grow upright to 100 x 60 cm (40 x 24 in), and have a some-what 'high-shouldered' appearance because the foliage clothes their upper parts so well.

'Silver Jubilee' was named for Queen Elizabeth II in her Jubilee year, and won the major award in St Albans in 1977, followed by Gold Medals in Belfast and Portland, and, in 1985, the very first James Mason award, to 'the rose that has given most pleasure during the past fifteen years'.
COCKER 1978.

Silver Jubilee

SIMBA GOLDSMITH, HELMUT SCHMIDT, KORbelma

Large-flowered hybrid tea bush

A good flower of 'Simba' is hard to beat, whether in the garden or cut for the house or for the show bench. The colour is an even shade of yellow, the flower form is perfect, and they present themselves to view on firm stems, on neat-growing plants, 60 x 50 cm (24 x 20 in). The German breeder decided this was good enough to name for the Chancellor of his country, but for the US it can be 'Goldsmith' or 'Helmut Schmidt' and in Britain they call it 'Simba'. Mark Mattock, the breeder's agent, relates that soon after a visit to Kenya his family acquired a Golden Labrador puppy. They called it Simba, which is the Swahili word for 'lion'. In Mark's words, 'This name seemed appropriate for the rose, which went from strength to strength. But sadly the puppy did not.'
KORDES 1981.

Simba

TEQUILA SUNRISE BEAULIEU, DICobey

Large-flowered hybrid tea bush

With a succession of flowers in yellow rimmed with scarlet, this brightens up the dullest days of summer, though it prefers the sun, as rain can cause pink spots on the outer petals of the rounded, cupped blooms. The colourful display, with flowers borne in wide sprays, continues to the autumn. The growth is bushy, with dark glossy leaves, to 75 x 60 cm (30 x 24 in). It has won Gold Medals in Belfast and St Albans.
DICKSON 1989.

Troika

Tequila Sunrise

TROIKA ROYAL DANE

Large-flowered hybrid tea bush

This produces consistently good blooms in a blend of reddish-orange with yellow and pink. They are fragrant, large and well formed with high centres, good for bedding, cutting and exhibition. Growth is strong and free branching to 90 x 75 cm (36 x 30 in) with good cover from the large, deep-green leaves. Its first Gold Medal (in memory of James Mason) came after twenty-one years in commerce, which may or may not be a record but is certainly evidence of its quality and stamina.
POULSEN 1972.

CLUSTER-FLOWERED (FLORIBUNDA) BUSH ROSES

AMBER QUEEN   PRINZ EUGEN VON SAVOYEN, HARroony

Cluster-flowered floribunda bush

The harvest of international prizes for this rose (twenty-six of them to date) indicate it must have special qualities. They are its pure amber-yellow colour; ability to produce big clusters of perfectly formed blooms freely over a long period; neat bedding habit; handsome and plentiful foliage, reddish when young; and sweet fragrance. It usually grows to about 50 x 60 cm (20 x 24 in). It was to have borne the name 'Rosemary Harkness', but when it won Britain's Rose of the Year competition, a change was made on grounds of general commercial acceptability. In Austria they had their own ideas and bestowed on it the name of a national hero instead.
HARKNESS 1984.

Amber Queen

Anne Harkness

ANNE HARKNESS HARkaramel

Cluster-flowered floribunda bush

This is a popular choice for Britain's amateur exhibitors, who grow and stage it to perfection, especially in the autumn. It lends itself to this purpose by producing spectacular sprays on long firm stems, each small bloom well filled with petals and exquisitely formed. Indeed, so much plant energy goes into them that they rarely open until well past midsummer, giving a useful splash of colour (and a resource for cutting) at a time when other garden roses are out of flower. The colour is a refreshing apricot-yellow and growth upright and strong to 120 x 60 cm (48 x 24 in). The rose was named for the elder daughter of Peter Harkness to mark her twenty-first birthday.
HARKNESS 1980.

CHAMPAGNE COCKTAIL HORflash

Cluster-flowered floribunda bush

Here is a rose to surprise your friends, for the combination of light yellow-flecked pink, with reverse deeper pink, is both unusual and variable, so that one is never exactly sure what the next blooms will bring. They are pleasantly scented, and borne in open clusters of large double blooms 9 cm (3.5 in) across – often more like hybrid teas than floribundas. The growth is upright, 100 x 70 cm (40 x 28 in), with a reasonable cover of dark leaves. This rose won a Gold Medal in the Glasgow Trials in 1990.
HORNER 1985.

Champagne Cocktail

Christopher Columbus

CHRISTOPHER COLUMBUS POUlstripe

Cluster-flowered floribunda bush

For lovers of the bizarre, this rose gives a new twist to the stripy roses. On a blush background appear heavy markings of cerise, which are well displayed on the wide-opening semi-double blooms. The plants grow bushily to 70 x 75 cm (28 x 30 in) with a background of plentiful dark foliage. Named for the 500th anniversary of Columbus's landfall in what he thought were islands off the coast of India. Rosarians may also be confused because there were two roses named for this occasion. One is from Meilland, but this one is by Poulsen 1992.
POULSEN 1992.

CITY OF BELFAST <small>MACci</small>

Cluster-flowered floribunda bush

City of Belfast

This makes an excellent bedding rose, with well filled clusters of scarlet blooms making a bold splash of colour, and good repeat flowering from summer to autumn. The leaves are glossy and the plants have a bushy habit, 60 cm (24 in) tall and wide. The variety was awarded the top prize in the British rose trials in 1967, and Gold Medals in New Zealand, Belfast and The Hague, abundant evidence of its superb quality. It has not perhaps had the commercial reward its merits deserve, possibly due to the breeder's later success with 'Trumpeter' in a similar colour.
MCGREDY 1968.

CITY OF LONDON <small>HARukfore</small>

Cluster-flowered floribunda bush
(also a shrub or climber)

Sweet scent, simple form and delicate blush tints give this the character of an old Bourbon rose; it was indeed exhibited as 'an unknown old garden rose' at a recent British Rose Festival. The clusters of blooms are produced on rather lax stems, which in mild climates enable it to be grown as a climber. It will normally grow to 80 x 75 cm (32 x 30 in), or up to 1.8 x 1.5 m (80 x 60 in) with support. It has received Gold Medals in Le Roeulx and The Hague, and was named to mark the 800th anniversary of the granting of London's charter, by Richard I.
HARKNESS 1988.

City of London

Disco Dancer

DISCO DANCER DICinfra

Cluster-flowered floribunda bush

A bed of 'Disco Dancer' in full bloom is just about the most dazzling sight in the rose garden. The bright orange-scarlet blooms are neatly spaced in big wide sprays, backed up by plentiful glossy foliage. It grows bushily to 75 x 60 cm (30 x 24 in). DICKSON 1984.

FELLOWSHIP LIVIN' EASY, HARwelcome

Cluster-flowered floribunda bush

The impression of this rose is one of plenty. It has an abundance of stems and leaves, and produces big clusters of sizeable flowers, deep orange with lighter flushes, freely through summer and autumn. There is pleasing scent, and it makes a fine bed or group, growing to 75 x 60 cm (30 x 24 in). 'Fellowship' is named for Rotary International and has received Gold Medals from St Albans and The Hague and the All America Rose Selection award.
HARKNESS 1992.

Fellowship

FLAIR DICrelax

Cluster-flowered floribunda bush

Flair

The cheerful clusters of canary-yellow flowers flushed with red make a good show from summer to autumn. This did well in the breeders' trials in Britain, where its neat leafy habit makes it useful for containers and small spaces. It grows to 45 cm (18 in) high and wide.
DICKSON 1993.

Frensham

FRENSHAM

Cluster-flowered floribunda bush

This was called a hybrid polyantha at the time of its introduction, for the word floribunda was not then in use. It was a postwar sensation, bearing its rich crimson blooms against a sea of foliage for many months, almost without a pause. The bud formation, slim and prettily furled, has particular appeal.

For ten years this remained the British market leader in what by then had become the floribunda class, then it suffered a steep decline as mildew dimmed the brilliance of the shiny leaflets. Some believe insufficient pruning was the cause, since the plants, left to themselves, make more foliage than they can support during dry spells in summer. Certainly they seem less troubled when subjected to hard pruning. The growth is heavily thorned, shrubby and dense to 120 x 90 cm (4 x 3 ft), and the variety received a Gold Medal from Britain's National Rose Society in 1943. The amateur raiser named it after the Surrey town close to his home.
NORMAN 1946.

FRIESIA SUNSPRITE, KORRESIA

Cluster-flowered floribunda bush

The delights of this rose are its bright yellow colour, sweet scent, good bedding habit and usefulness for cutting. The form of the bloom is unusual, for the young flowers hold their centres while the outer petals unfold, with wavy edges. The growth is bushy to 75 x 60 cm (30 x 24 in). Gold Medals from Baden-Baden in 1972 and St Albans in 1989 attest its long-term popularity. But why three names? 'Sunsprite' is used in the US, and 'Friesia' in many countries, but in Britain the growers obey a horticultural rule that a rose name should not carry the name of another type of flower. The only floribunda to receive The Gamble Award for fragrance. KORDES 1974.

Iceberg

ICEBERG FÉE DES NEIGES, SCHNEEWITTCHEN, KORbin

Cluster-flowered floribunda bush

The merits of this rose are summed up by Jack Harkness's comment: 'What a pity we don't have an "Iceberg" in every colour; there would be no need to grow a long list of floribundas then.'

For a white rose to be a best seller and enter the Hall of Fame as one of the world's favourites is remarkable, since white is supposed to be an 'uncommercial colour'. Among its virtues are freedom of bloom, the pleasing way the flowers are disposed in each truss, a neat rounded habit, and bright abundant foliage. The old flower petals drop cleanly and the colour tone is fresh and cheering on the dullest of days; in hot weather, the petals may become flecked with pink. 'Iceberg' grows to 80 x 65 cm (32 x 26 in), or bigger if lightly pruned. Curiously it has one noticeable fault: rabbits are partial to the light shiny leaves. Gold Medals were awarded in Baden-Baden and St Albans in 1958.
KORDES 1958.

Lili Marlene

LILI MARLENE   KORlima

Cluster-flowered floribunda bush

For many years, beds of this deep-scarlet-red variety with its showy clusters of bloom have been extensively plant-ed in gardens and pub-lic parks. It maintains a neat, leafy, bushy habit, 70 x 60 cm (28 x 24 in). In The Hague, where suitability for parks use shows up in the trials, it received the coveted Golden Rose. In the Second World War, the song of this name became a popular theme for the armies of both sides. KORDES 1959.

MARGARET MERRIL   HARkuly

Cluster-flowered floribunda bush

At some shows you will see a class for 'Three-Stage Roses'. This calls for a bud, a perfect bloom (half to three-quarters open) and a full bloom (fully open, with the stamens fresh) to be staged. There are a few roses that look superb in all three stages, and

Margaret Merril

'Margaret Meriril' is among them. The flowers are blush to white, shaped like hybrid teas and very fragrant. A bloom or two cut for the house can scent the room, and they have a good vase life. Sometimes they bloom in a cluster, some-times singly. Growth is upright to 80 x 60 cm (32 x 24 in) with an adequate cover of dark, leathery leaves; they are not always proof against seasonal black spot. Five Gold Medals and a clutch of fragrance awards are evidence of the pleasure this variety gives. The only sad note is that Margaret Merril as a person does not actually exist! It was a name dreamed up by the makers of Oil of Ulay, who com-missioned the rose, for their Beauty Adviser.

HARKNESS 1977.

MATANGI MACman

Cluster-flowered floribunda bush

Bred from 'Picasso', this is one of the loveliest of the 'painted' roses, with petals of rich orange-red with a white eye, and silvery white on the reverse. These are borne in clusters against a background of dark glossy leaves to beautiful effect. The plants are neat and bushy in growth, 80 x 60 cm (32 x 24 in).

The New Zealand raiser says the name means different things to different people: it is a Maori word for 'breeze' and also a village name, and was the name of one of the first troopships bringing soldiers home after the Second World War. 'Matangi' has an impressive haul of awards, including Gold Medals in Belfast, Portland, Rome and St Albans.
MCGREDY 1974.

Matangi

Mountbatten

MOUNTBATTEN HARmantelle

Cluster-flowered shrub

This is a splendid choice for a rose hedge, or a large bed of one variety. The foliage is handsome, and indeed the crisp dark leaves persist well into winter. The raiser described it as his 'pagoda' rose, from the graceful way the flowers are borne at different levels on the plant. They are scented, mimosa-yellow, and open to a rounded shape with the outer petals reflexing and then incurving to give a chrysanthemum effect. Growth is upright to 120 x 75 cm (48 x 30 in). 'Mountbatten' was the first UK Rose of the Year, and winner of four Gold Medals. It honours the memory of Earl Mountbatten of Burma, 1900-79, under whose command the raiser served in the Second World War.
HARKNESS 1982.

NEWS LEGnews

Cluster-flowered floribunda bush

The remarkable beetroot-purple colour is the reason why this rose is grown, and it is well displayed in the big clusters of open blooms. They are scented and continue through summer and autumn, making 'News' a good bedding rose, though not easy to place in an overall planting scheme. The plants grow upright, with good dark leaves, to 60 x 50 cm (24 x 20 in). With full marks for novelty, this received the National Rose Society's Gold Medal in 1970. The breeder used a mauve variety 'Lilac Charm' and the gallica rose 'Tuscany Superb'.
LEGRICE 1968.

Old Master

OLD MASTER MACesp

Cluster-flowered floribunda bush

The flowers show carmine shades and markings on a white background, this being yet another byblow of the 'painted roses' breeding work. It has large blooms for a floribunda, 11 cm (4.5 in) across. The growth is bushy, to 80 x 60 cm (32 x 24 in). MCGREDY 1974.

PLAYBOY CHEERIO

Cluster-flowered floribunda bush

Life is full of surprises, and the Scottish breeder looking at this rose among his unnamed seedlings would hardly imagine that with only a few petals it could become popular in a climate like that of California; yet so it proved. The colours are a melange of orange-yellow shaded scarlet, well displayed as the blooms open in big sprays. The continuity of bloom is excellent. The plants grow bushy, with plentiful dark glossy foliage to 75 x 65 cm (30 x 26 in). After thirteen years in commerce, 'Playboy' received its first Gold Medal, from Portland USA. COCKER 1976.

Playboy

Playgirl

PLAYGIRL   MORplag

Cluster-flowered floribunda bush

The success of 'Playboy' has encouraged the emergence of an excellent pink counterpart, with similar flower form, showing golden stamens as it opens out. In habit of growth and general effect it resembles the earlier variety, and they make suitable partners in a bed.
MOORE 1986.

Pride of Maldon

PRIDE OF MALDON   HARwonder

Cluster-flowered floribunda bush

This rose is notable for producing flowers repeatedly through the summer and autumn months. They are semi-double, with lively reddish orange on the inside of the petals, and yellow on the reverse, a vibrant combination. The foliage is glossy, dark and plentiful, and the habit very bushy to 75 x 60 cm (30 x 24 in).

Maldon is an ancient port in Essex, scene of an epic battle between Saxon and Dane in 991, and the rose is named to celebrate its millennium.
HARKNESS 1991.

Princess Alice

PRINCESS ALICE   BRITE LITES, ZONTA ROSE, HARtanna

Cluster-flowered floribunda bush

A typical spray of this rose will comprise a score of bright yellow roses on slim, firm stems, so disposed as to form a natural floral bouquet. The flowers are good for cutting, and the plants are tall, enabling entire sprays to be cut if required for the house or exhibition. Grows upright to 110 x 60 cm (42 x 24 in). The name honours HRH Princess Alice, Duchess of Gloucester, a keen rosarian, and the rose has achieved top honours in Dublin and Orleans.
HARKNESS 1985.

RADOX BOUQUET ROSIKA, HARmusky

Cluster-flowered floribunda bush

Radox Bouquet

This is like an old centifolia rose in modern dress, as the richly fragrant, full-petalled, sometimes quartered pink flowers are accompanied by today's typical handsome shiny leaves. The flowers are lovely to cut, and continue to appear through summer and autumn on upright, shrubby plants, 90 x 60 cm (3 x 2 ft). The variety holds fragrance awards from Belfast and Geneva, much to the delight of the Radox company, for whom it was named.
HARKNESS 1981.

REGENSBERG BUFFALO BILL, YOUNG MISTRESS, MACyoumis

Cluster-flowered floribunda bush

This rose puts tremendous energy into making flowers at the expense of growth, making it ideal for the front of a border or for a bed where short plants are appropriate. The full-petalled blooms are deep pink, patterned with white, opening up to 11 cm (4.5 in) across, which is large in proportion to the size of plant. Indeed, the plants are almost hidden from sight at peak flowering time. The foliage is glossy and effectively clothes the 40 x 50 cm (16 x 20 in) bushes. This is a rose that attracts the eye; it did so in the Baden-Baden trials, where the judges awarded a Gold Medal.
MCGREDY 1979.

Regensberg

116

SEXY REXY HECKENZAUBER, MACrexy

Cluster-flowered floribunda bush

The pretty camellia-style blooms are borne in clusters so densely packed that they conceal most of the plant at peak flowering time. They are a warm shade of rose pink, and nestle closely against the glossy foliage on plants of bushy, even habit, 70 x 60 cm (28 x 24 in). The variety's merits have earned it Gold Medals in New Zealand, Scotland and the US, and it is named for a friend of Sam McGredy, who introduced it in 1984.
MCGREDY 1984.

Sexy Rexy

SHEILA'S PERFUME   HARsherry

Cluster-flowered floribunda bush (in some countries known as a large-flowered hybrid tea bush rose)

Many breeders were keen to produce a healthy bicolour red and yellow rose with scent. That this feat was performed by an amateur, raising his seedlings on a London windowsill, shows how good fortune can attend those who make the effort. The rose makes an attractive dark-foliaged plant, with a good succession of fragrant, full-petalled flowers opening out from pretty urn-shaped buds. The blooms are of good size and the variety is quite just-ifiably listed as a hybrid tea by some. Growth is bushy, 75 x 60 cm (30 x 24 in), and the scent of the flowers has been rewarded by the judges in St Albans, Glasgow, and more recently in New Zealand. John Sheridan named it for his wife and it was introduced in 1985. SHERIDAN 1985.

Sheila's Perfume

TANGO   ROCK 'N' ROLL, STRETCH JOHNSON, MACfirwal

Cluster-flowered floribunda bush

The attraction of this rose lies in its novel colouring. On the inside, the petals are orange-scarlet with a whitish rim and yellow base, and they are light yellow on the reverse. As they appear in clusters of many medium-sized semi-double blooms, the effect is indeed eye-catching. The plants are leafy and grow upright to 75 x 60 cm (30 x 24 in). This rose of several aliases was bred from 'Sexy Rexy' x 'Maestro' by McGredy, and received a Gold Medal in St Albans in its year of introduction, 1988. MCGREDY 1988.

Tango

Trumpeter

TRUMPETER MACtru

Cluster-flowered floribunda bush

This rose is splendid for a bed or hedge where a short neat plant is required. It certainly trumpets its presence with showy sprays of bright orange-scarlet flowers, freely produced from summer to autumn. It is a leafy, bushy grower, to 60 x 50 cm (24 x 20 in), and has won well deserved Gold Medals in New Zealand, the US and Britain.
MCGREDY 1977.

PATIO AND MINIATURE ROSES

Anna Ford

ANNA FORD HARpiccolo

Dwarf cluster-flowered patio bush

This may well come to be considered the first of the modern patio roses, because it fulfils very well the subsequent definition of these as being like scaled-down versions of bushes with every plant part in proportion. In the US, where the patio class is not recognised, it would be known as a miniature. The flowers are carried in showy clusters close to the small polished leaves, in a lively orange-red hue with yellow at the base. Individually they lay claim to no special beauty, but their value lies in their massed colour effect and the constancy with which they are produced from summer to late autumn. The growth is bushy, 45 x 40 cm (18 x 15 in). Anna Ford, well known from British television, chose this rose to bear her name on a visit to Chelsea Show. It won the highest award in the British Rose Trials in 1981, plus Gold Medals in Genoa and Glasgow.
HARKNESS 1980.

CIDER CUP   DICladida

Dwarf cluster-flowered patio bush

For a small space where a neat upright plant is required, this is a highly desirable garden item. It seems hardly ever out of flower from summer to autumn, bearing a succession of modest-sized, prettily formed deep-apricot-pink blooms in clusters on bushy upright plants, 45 x 30 cm (18 x 12 in). This rose was named on behalf of a newspaper in Somerset, the home of good cider. It is now available on the US market, where it is classified as a miniature.
DICKSON 1988.

CONSERVATION   COCdimple

Dwarf cluster-flowered patio bush

Conservation

This is one of the best roses for continuity of bloom. Each flower is made up of reddish-pink petals with yellow centres, and as they are produced in wide clusters they create a most showy effect. The growth is bushy, 45 x 45 cm (18 x 18 in), and the leaves small and glossy, and rather attractive to rabbits; since this is named for the Worldwide Fund for Nature one can hardly complain about that. It received a Gold Medal in the Dublin Trials.
COCKER 1988.

Cider Cup

Cottage Garden

COTTAGE GARDEN   HARyamber

Dwarf cluster-flowered patio bush

For gardens where space is limited, the patio roses are most useful. This one is upright and colourful, with deep apricot blooms opening like zinnias, or sometimes quartered, backed by leathery dark foliage. It has an upright habit to 60 x 45 cm (24 x 18 in). The name derives from Garden House Hospice (formerly a Cottage Hospital) in N Herts, England, for which it was named. HARKNESS 1992.

Emily Louise

EMILY LOUISE HARwilla

Dwarf cluster-flowered patio bush

The unusual features of this rose are its simple starry yellow flowers, which go brownish with age and are constantly being produced through summer and autumn, and the leaves, as black in the young stage as you will find on any rose. It has a low, spreading habit, 45 cm (18 in) tall and wide.

It commemorates a four-year-old who died in very tragic circumstances, and whose favourite flower was the rose. It is bred from 'Judy Garland' x 'Anna Ford'. HARKNESS 1990.

FIGURINE BENfig

Miniature bush

Visitors to shows often see this variety entered, and winning first prize. Long elegant buds open into prettily formed ivory-white flowers, with a tinge of pink; they are carried sometimes singly, sometimes in clusters, and are good for cutting. Grows bushy and upright, and bigger than most miniatures, to 60 x 40 cm (24 x 18 in).
BENARDELLA 1991.

Figurine

GOOD AS GOLD CHEWSUNBEAM

Miniature climber

Good As Gold

One of the most recent rose developments has been the advent of a group of climbers of restrained growth in which the flowers and leaves are miniaturised. These are enabling gardeners to cover modest structures with plants that will not get out of hand, yet give optimum flower impact. 'Good as Gold' produces sizeable clusters of petite bright-yellow blooms with a hint of fragrance. It grows upright to 2.5 x 1.2 m (8 x 4 ft) with a plentiful covering of small, dark, shiny leaflets.

The rose is bred by Chris Warner, who has received several major awards for these novel climbers; he prefers to call them patio climbers. Whatever we call it, it's a lovely free-flowering garden rose, though it can be hard to find in the US.

WARNER, 1995.

MARLENA

Dwarf cluster-flowered patio bush

This short-growing rose is ideal for a bed or low hedge where space is limited. It bears clusters of cupped dark crimson blooms, lightened with paler crimson, in great profusion from summer to autumn; at times they almost hide the dark green leaves. The growth is neat and bushy, 45 cm (18 in) tall and wide. This has won Gold Medals in Baden-Baden and Belfast, and is said to be named for Marlene Dietrich.
KORDES 1964.

Marlena

Queen Mother

QUEEN MOTHER   KORquemu

Dwarf cluster-flowered patio shrub
(in some countries known as a cluster-flowered, or floribunda,
bush rose or a shrub)

Where a low, spreading but compact rose is wanted in the garden – or in a tub – this serves the purpose very well. It has semi-double blooms of clear pink, borne in wide clusters so that they appear scattered on the bush; they open out flat, displaying the stamens to charming effect. The flowering continues until late in the season, almost without a break. The plant is well furnished with shiny, rather small, almost evergreen leaves, and grows unevenly to about 40 x 60 cm (16 x 24 in). Limited availability in the US.
KORDES 1991.

SI

Miniature bush

Si

Sean McCann considers this the smallest of the miniatures, which makes its name – the shortest of any rose – very appropriate. It has light pink to blush-white flowers on plants described as 'micro-mini', up to 15 cm (8 in) high, which continue to give a good show of bloom through summer and autumn. The plant is neatly furnished with pointed petite leaflets.
DOT 1957.

STACEY SUE

Miniature bush

Stacey Sue

The search for perfection goes on, and this rose has such moments, when the rose-pink flowers, neatly arrayed by nature's hand, nestle against the crisp green leaves. The blooms are full of short petals, and open like dainty rosettes. The growth is low, bushy, 25 x 30 cm (10 x 12 in). Ralph Moore raised this and named it for one of his grand-daughters. It was introduced in 1976.

SWEET MAGIC   DICmagic

Dwarf cluster-flowered patio bush

Sweet Magic

This is one of the prettiest patio roses, orange with golden tints, and though the blooms are small, they make a good display, opening in clusters against a background of dainty, bright leaves. The habit is neat and bushy, 35 cm (14 in) high and wide. There is an appreciable scent – if you can get down that far.

'Sweet Magic' tied with 'Royal William' on a show of hands in a contest to choose the Rose of the Year for 1987. A postal ballot was arranged so that absentees could vote, and to everyone's surprise it yielded the same result. Both roses were therefore promoted, and both have proved their worth.
DICKSON 1987.

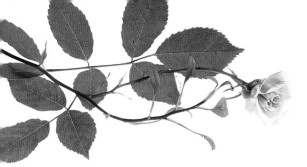

INDEX